Original title:
Woodland Wordsmith

Copyright © 2025 Creative Arts Management OÜ
All rights reserved.

Author: Julian Montgomery
ISBN HARDBACK: 978-1-80567-260-9
ISBN PAPERBACK: 978-1-80567-559-4

Narrative in the Nightshade

In the shadows where whispers play,
The mushrooms gossip in a silly way.
A hedgehog wears a tiny crown,
As the owl hoots, "Don't you frown!"

The fireflies dance with buzzing glee,
Chasing each other 'round the old tree.
A badger spins tales of brave quests,
While crickets chirp with silly jest.

Lyrics from the Lichen

On the bark, the lichen sings,
Of bounce and wiggle, of odd things.
A squirrel joins with a playful cheer,
Waving his tail, a furry seer.

The frogs croak out a catchy beat,
While beetles tap their tiny feet.
A snail draws lines in smooth delight,
In a waltz under the moonlight.

The Quill and the Quercus

In the hollow of a grand old oak,
A quill sits laughing, joking the folk.
With acorns rolling, they start a race,
The laughter echoes, a merry space.

The raccoons gather for a grand show,
Imitating each other, moving slow.
The wind whispers secrets, oh so sly,
As the sun bids the day goodbye.

Poems in the Pine Breeze

In the breeze, the pine trees sway,
Rustling words in a cheeky way.
A porcupine pens a witty rhyme,
Tickling the air, passing the time.

The squirrels tease with their clever tricks,
Dropping pinecones, throwing quick licks.
The sun peeks through with a giggle bright,
As day turns to fun in the soft twilight.

Sprouts of Starlit Stories

In the forest, twinkling lights,
Squirrels gossip, sharing sights.
Frogs recite their jumpy tales,
Bouncing beats and chirpy wails.

Owls wear glasses, wise and round,
While rabbits hop without a sound.
Each leaf whispers a secret tune,
As raccoons dance beneath the moon.

Nature's Testament

The trees hold court, a leafy crew,
Claiming wisdom, saying, "Who knew?"
A hedgehog scribbles with a pen,
Writing tales of wily men.

Beneath the roots, a joke takes shape,
Where fungi laugh, all cloaked in tape.
Badgers play cards beside a brook,
While fireflies glow, and crickets cook.

Whimsy in the Wild Foliage

A bushy-tailed fox wore a hat,
Declaring to all, "I'm where it's at!"
Lazily lounging on a big log,
Dreaming of pies, a sweet food blog.

The berries giggle as they grow,
Winking at bees that buzz to and fro.
Sunbeams tickle the branches high,
As the clouds float by with a sigh.

Rhyme among the Roots

Deep in the earth, the worms hold shows,
Each one reciting, wearing bright clothes.
Ants hum along with a rhythmic beat,
   As beetles tap dance on tiny feet.

Mice munch on words like they're popcorn,
Happy to share both laughter and scorn.
The leaves join in, rustling with glee,
   In this forest bash, wild and free.

Stanzas of the Starlit Clearing

Under the moon, raccoons play pranks,
Squirrel debates with a skunk in the ranks.
Owls giggle softly, sharing their notes,
While rabbits gather in secretive coats.

Stars wink above in a twinkly jest,
Each creature thinking they're truly the best.
Fireflies buzz with a flicker and flare,
Draw maps of laughter that fill up the air.

The Prose of Pathway Shadows

The toadstools gossip with their little caps,
Frogs tell tall tales of exploring mishaps.
A hedgehog pens stories, quills all a-fluff,
While beetles debate who's got the best stuff.

In shadows they linger, plotting their pranks,
Twirling around in imaginary ranks.
With whispers and chuckles, the path comes alive,
In the dappled light where giggles survive.

Lines from the Luminous Glade

In the glade where giggles grow,
Laughter leaps from toe to toe.
A parrot squawks with rhymes so absurd,
While a chipmunk hums every silly word.

The trees sway gently, clapping their leaves,
As squirrels compose on their tiny eves.
Each branch a stage for a comedy show,
As critters join in with their quirkiest flow.

The Scribe of Swirling Mist

A turtle's slow tales swirl in the breeze,
While a rabbit writes once upon a sneeze.
Foxes with feathers pen stories of flight,
In foggy whispers they dance through the night.

The mist carries giggles from tree to tree,
As all woodland creatures join in with glee.
With scribbles and squiggles they make quite a scene,
In a swirl of laughter, like dreams evergreen.

Echoes of the Elder Trees

In the shade where squirrels race,
And whispers tickle leaves' face.
The owls hoot a clever tune,
As acorns fall like soft balloons.

Mushrooms dance in sprightly glee,
Chasing shadows, wild and free.
The pinecones giggle, what a sight,
As rabbits join the game tonight.

Beneath the branches, jokes abound,
The branches sway like laughter's sound.
Foxes tell tales on starlit logs,
While frogs play cards with absent dogs.

A breeze sweeps by with playful glee,
Spreading laughter through every tree.
Nature's humor, oh so grand,
In this happy forest land.

The Flute of the Foliage

Amidst the leaves, a whistle blows,
A melody that tickles toes.
The bees hum tunes in perfect time,
While ants join in with a silly rhyme.

Squirrels strut with flutes so fine,
Crafted from the tallest pine.
Each note a spark, a laugh, a cheer,
As butterflies twirl, drawing near.

The raccoons tap on hollow logs,
Jamming out with all the frogs.
The underbrush shakes with jests,
As nature holds her merry fest.

In the hush of the twilight air,
A symphony without a care.
Join the dance, let laughter flow,
In this music, joy will grow.

Poetic Prowess in the Pines

Amidst the trunks of feisty green,
The poets craft with humor keen.
Each rhyme a twist, a quirky jest,
Nature's wit put to the test.

Chirping robins share their rhymes,
As laughter echoes through the times.
The chipmunks pen their comic verse,
In the poetry of the universe.

The wind drafts lines with gentle strokes,
While wise old trees crack gentle jokes.
Tails and tales all intertwine,
In the forest's frolic, all is fine.

So gather round in leafy shade,
Let's share the laughs that nature made.
With every line, a giggle shared,
In this wild world, none are scared.

Verses by the Verdant Veldt

In the forest where squirrels play,
They steal my snacks, oh what a day!
I shout and chase, they think it's fun,
They taunt me back; I can't quite run.

The rabbits giggle as they hop,
Ensuring my lunch just might drop.
With grass in my hair, I take a seat,
As the rascals munch my tasty treat.

Birds above in feathers bright,
Sing tunes that make the trees take flight.
They mimic me, oh what a voice,
I join their choir, I've lost my choice.

Yet in this laughter, I find my glee,
For nature's jesters are wild and free.
In the shade, I bid the sun farewell,
And hug the trees, they know me well.

Narrative Nooks of Nature

In a nook where the fables twine,
The owls wear glasses; they think they're fine.
They tell me stories of stars and moons,
While raccoons dance to peculiar tunes.

There's a squirrel with a crown made of leaves,
Declaring monarchy, who believes?
He orders acorns from his high throne,
But birds just giggle and loudly groan.

A badger writes tales with a pen of grass,
His tales leave me laughing, oh what a class!
Each story twists like a winding stream,
And ends with a creature who lost his dream.

In these nooks, the giggles swell,
Nature's jester rings the bell.
So here's a toast; raise your cup high,
To tales of mischief that never die!

The Letter of the Lynx

The lynx sat down with a quill and ink,
To write a letter; oh, what do you think?
He wrote to the fox, with a giggle and glee,
Inviting him over for woodland tea.

But the fox wrote back, in a snarky sort,
"Can you bake pastries? I prefer dessert!"
The lynx frowned then pondered quite hard,
"I'll leave out the nuts; I might lose my card."

Then hedgehogs joined, with a pun or two,
"Let's roll a party; that sounds fun to do!"
They brought out the pie and shared in delight,
Laughter rang out through the cool moonlight.

The letter's clear, not just ink on a page,
It's friendship's hug, and a bold, funny stage.
So here's to the lynx, with his thoughtful surprise,
In the heart of the woods, where hilarity flies!

The Grove's Golden Gleanings

Beneath the boughs of the ancient trees,
I found some treasures caught in the breeze.
A pinecone wearing a tiny hat,
An acorn that danced with a nearby cat.

The mushrooms debated their own big fame,
"Are we delicious, or is it just lame?"
While a porcupine juggled some twigs in the air,
He tripped on his quills; oh, couldn't beware!

A stumpy frog croaked with glee,
"Let's throw a bash, just come honor me!"
With petals as plates and grass as the floor,
They feasted on laughter; who could ask for more?

So in this grove, where the funny unfolds,
My heart fills with joy; let their story be told.
For nature's absurdity brings endless delight,
In golden gleanings, all through the night.

The Lullaby of Leafy Boughs

Swaying branches whisper low,
Even squirrels put on a show.
A leaf drops with a silly plop,
The laughter, oh, it just won't stop!

Fat acorns dance on the ground,
What a silly sight they've found!
With every tumble and every roll,
The laughter's creeping up your soul!

Breezes tickle trees up high,
As birds below just watch and sigh.
In this leafy world, we cheer,
For joy is rolling, never fear!

So next time when you take a stroll,
Hear the giggles in the shoal.
It's nature's joke, just take a pause,
And join the fun without a cause!

Echoes Beneath the Ferns

Beneath the fronds where shadows play,
A frog leaps up, what a display!
His croak's a tune, a silly beat,
A chorus sung by smelly feet!

The rabbits dance, they twirl and spin,
In froggy choirs, they join in.
With every hop, they bounce and laugh,
And miss their snacks, oh what a gaff!

A turtle thinks he's part of the show,
Pretends to dance in very slow.
The ferns are shaking with delight,
At this oddball party, what a sight!

So when you wander, take a glance,
At nature's quirky, wobbly dance.
For echoes here tell tales of glee,
In a ferny world, come join the spree!

The Muse of Moss-Covered Stones

Mossy stones sit with a grin,
Spinning stories we shouldn't win.
They whisper jokes from days long past,
With every tick, the moments last.

A ladybug swears it's the king,
While snails mock his not-so-zippy bling.
They slide on moss in a regal way,
A court of critters at their play!

Moss-covered stones with moods so grand,
Tell secrets fate more misconstrued and planned.
With every riddle, every pun,
Nature's laughter has just begun!

So bend your ear, and join the jest,
Among the stones, you'll feel the best.
For every laugh, and every tease,
Brings smiles and joy, a subtle breeze!

Ballet of the Bramble

In brambly bounds where shadows dart,
Thorns wear tiaras, oh, what art!
Berries giggle, red and sweet,
As bushes samba on their feet!

Thistles pirouette with a twist,
While beetles throw their arms and insist.
The hedgehogs cheer with fluffy pride,
In this wild dance, they all confide!

A bumblebee leads with a buzz so bright,
He sways and swirls in pure delight.
The bramble twirls, a leafy spree,
A ballet that's free, so wild and free!

So when you stroll through thicket fair,
Listen close, feel the flair.
For in this dance of thorn and bloom,
Life's a riot, in nature's room!

Riddles of the Rustic Glade

In the glade where giggles dwell,
Mushrooms dance and squirrels yell.
Who stole the acorn? Was it you?
Blame the rabbit, he's in on the view.

Under a tree, a wise old crow,
Says, "Guess my riddle, if you know!"
What has a tail but cannot wag?
A feathered friend, that loves to brag!

The berries chuckle, all in a line,
"Eat us, eat us! We taste just fine!"
But the fox rolls his eyes with a smirk,
"I'd rather chase than do this work!"

Laughter echoes through every breeze,
As branches sway and tickle your knees.
In this enchanted, silly space,
Even the leaves jump in a race!

Inkwells of the Meadow

In the meadow, amid blooms bright,
A bunny scribbles with pure delight.
His pencil's a carrot, his paper, a leaf,
His doodles spark laughter, bring joy, and relief.

The ants get together, each one with a quill,
Writing stories of crumbs, "What a thrill!"
But when they read, all they see is cheese,
Turns out their ink was just some breeze!

Mice hold a meeting, with cheese on the side,
Praising the stories that their friends tried.
But someone squeaks, "A tale went wrong,
The cat chased our tales, singing its song!"

Flowers giggle, swaying in rhyme,
"Let's write a tale of living in time!"
With pencils of petals and inks of dew,
The meadow's a canvas, so fresh and new!

Tales Told by Twigs

Two twigs sit snug on a branch so high,
Swapping their stories, oh my, oh my!
One claims, "I once went to the moon,"
The other replies, "Brought back a tune!"

A leaf nearby chuckles, makes a bet,
"Twigs can't travel, don't you forget!"
But they laugh back, "We've seen it all,
From screaming storms to the springtime call!"

Suddenly a breeze joins the fun,
Whisp'ring tales of how leaves come undone.
"Have you seen me do the spin?" it laughs,
As twigs dance along, do goofy half-staffs!

The sun beams down, a glittering friend,
Each twig's story doth seem to blend.
With giggles and grins, they twirl and twine,
In this world of whimsy, they truly shine!

Chronicles of the Leafy Realm

In a leafy realm where shadows hide,
A snail tells tales with excessive pride.
"Speed is my game, just you wait and see,"
But takes him two hours to cross a tree!

There's gossip afoot among the grass,
"Did you hear about the tortoise, alas?
He raced through puddles, fell in a splash,
Claimed he was swimming, but oh what a crash!"

A butterfly flutters, making a fuss,
"I wrote a poem, come read it to us!"
But all they see is her dancing around,
A flit-flap of colors, without a sound!

With every chuckle, the day drifts by,
Beetles are laughing as fireflies fly.
In this quirky realm, with stories to tell,
Nature's joy rings out—oh, can't you tell?

Inked in the Ivy

In the vines where tales get spun,
A squirrel winks, he's having fun.
With acorns stacked, a writer's prize,
He drafts a joke, weaves laughter's ties.

The owl hoots, he's quite the bard,
Spinning verses, ever charred.
His jokes are dry, his puns a flop,
But we can't help but laugh and hop.

In shady nooks where giggles roll,
A rabbit claims he's on a stroll.
Writes limericks with a twitching nose,
'Bout carrots wearing fancy clothes!

With every leaf, a chuckle finds,
Silly critters, clever minds.
In ivy's grasp, where laughs entwine,
A symphony of fun divine!

Prologues of the Ponderosa

Bears in bows, they write their lore,
Naming trees, and so much more.
Each ponderosa, tall and grand,
Holds tales of pranks, both sly and planned.

Chipmunks scribble on the bark,
With tiny pens, they leave a mark.
A saga of nuts, and forest greens,
Their epic quests blend laughs and beans!

Write a line, an owl's soft caw,
Mice giggle, hiding from the claw.
They pen their fears in rhymes so neat,
Of dodgeball games with crafty feet.

Under stars, the echoes ring,
In playful winds, the critters sing.
Stories dance upon the breeze,
In ponderosa, all hearts seize!

Words in the Wilderness

In a glen where chatter grows,
A bear recites with a booming prose.
His jokes so corny, they make us roar,
With punchlines hidden behind the door.

A raccoon flips through pages worn,
Finds tales of socks that run at dawn.
He giggles, curls up, oh what a sight,
In the wild, laughter takes flight.

The frogs croak rhymes, a leaping spree,
Each jump's a line, so wild and free.
With every splash, the pond concurs,
In wilderness, the laughter stirs.

Around the trees, the stories weave,
The more we share, the more we believe.
In every wink, in every verse,
The wilderness offers its playful curse!

Arachnid's Almanac

In corners where the cobwebs sway,
A spider spins his jokes all day.
His almanac of puns, so neat,
With tangled lines, a trickster's treat.

Fly caught in his webbed delight,
He giggles softly, oh what a sight!
"Don't worry friend, it's just a game,
With every buzz, it's all the same."

His silk holds tales of woe and fun,
He bakes them well under the sun.
Crafting stories with eight-legged grace,
In laughter's web, we find our place.

Like shadows that dance with whispers sweet,
In every twist, we find the beat.
An arachnid's almanac, a clever play,
Where chuckles flutter and pranks hold sway!

The Stanza of Stillness

In a forest of whispers, so sly and so hint,
The squirrels write novels with a flick of their mint.
Acorns as paper, and twigs as their quills,
Their stories are laughed at, giving everyone thrills.

The owls in their circles hold book clubs at night,
Discussing sharp plots with the moon as their light.
They review every tale with a hoot and a caw,
While raccoons sneak peeks, breaking every raw law.

Frogs act as agents, with toads as their stars,
Publishing tales of tree frogs with fancy guitars.
Their readers are fish, flipping pages with glee,
In the swamps, stories bounce, dancing wild and free.

So next time you're lost in a glade that feels shy,
Listen for laughter; just stop and ask why.
For in every nook, a new fable can sprout,
In the funny green pages where critters hang out.

Verses at the Vesper

As twilight tips over with tales yet untold,
The critters unite in a gathering bold.
Fireflies glow like little ink dots,
While frogs serenade with their ribbits and thoughts.

The hedgehogs have hats, and the rabbits wear ties,
Debating the best ways to outsmart the flies.
The trees are the witnesses, old and wise,
Listening closely with twinkling eyes.

A raccoon tells jokes, his paws on his knees,
Inquiring if trees like to dance in the breeze.
The salamanders chuckle, flipping jokes 'round,
While the crickets keep time with their chirps as their sound.

Thus verses take flight as the stars start to twirl,
In the gathering dusk, the laughter will swirl.
Each line is a flavor, a sweet, silly song,
Where the evening brings giggles, the whole night long.

Fables of the Fern Fronds

A family of ferns flirts with dainty fun,
Dancing with pixies beneath the warm sun.
They giggle at shadows that prance all around,
Creating a spree in the roots of the ground.

The elder tree whispers of tales from the past,
Of how leaves could chatter, their giggles amassed.
With vines as the scribes, and petals as ink,
Each fable told brings a wink and a blink.

Enemies of ivy and creeping yew trees,
Dare to tell stories of avoiding the bees.
Their tales are absurd, twisted bows and knits,
When they laugh, the whole glen shakes from their fits.

So wander with caution where ferns take their stand,
For laughter may tickle, and tickles expand.
In the kingdom of greens, where giggles are king,
Every frond is a page, let the chuckling ring!

Dreams on Dew-Kissed Petals

Petals hum softly with dreams in the night,
As ladybugs weave through the moon's gentle light.
With dewdrops like diamonds, they sparkle and gleam,
While butterflies chuckle at the silliness theme.

The daisies throw parties with shares of bright wit,
With jokes on their stems, they all merrily sit.
The bees bring the nectar, sweet black and gold,
For the best punchline that's ever been told.

In the garden, the blooms play a game of charades,
Pretending to be trees, or cool lemonade shades.
The tulips suggest they take flight for a while,
To join in the laughter, their petals all smile.

So dream on the petals, where giggles take flight,
In a patch where the flowers sing sweetly at night.
For the fun of the blooms is a whimsical play,
In a garden where joy shines the brightest of way.

The Tale Beneath the Treetops

In a forest where squirrels chatter,
A wise old owl's nose grows fatter.
He claims he writes the best of prose,
But rhymes come out with silly toes.

Beneath the shade, the acorns dance,
They hold a party, take a chance.
With hats made from the finest leaves,
They debate which nut trick or treat retrieves.

The fox, he thinks he's quite the bard,
But puns he delivers are way too hard.
Yet everyone laughs at his crazy schemes,
As they tumble down in giggling dreams.

So in the trees, the stories flow,
A merry troupe, a lively show.
With laughter echoing through the pines,
The creatures sing, oh how it shines!

Musing of the Mossy Knoll

Upon a knoll where dampness gleams,
The mushrooms gather, sharing dreams.
With tiny caps and shiny shoes,
They ponder why they still have dues.

A cheeky toad hops into view,
With witty lines that are all askew.
He boasts of leaps and how he flies,
Yet lands with plop, oh what a surprise!

Nearby, a hedgehog spins a tale,
Of epic quests that always fail.
His heroic jumps are rarely seen,
As all his stories slip between.

Yet laughter rings from every side,
As critters gather, fun their guide.
For on this knoll, with laughs like these,
Each day is light, a joy to seize!

The Poetry of Pollen

In a meadow alive with buzz,
The bees compose a verse because,
Their honey drips with humor sweet,
With sticky lines that can't be beat.

A flower stands, it strikes a pose,
With petals bright, but funny throes.
It sneezes pollen all around,
And makes a sneeze fest, quite profound.

The butterflies dance, a charming crew,
A ballet where the petals flew.
Each pirouette ends in a snicker,
As blooms turn redder from the snicker.

So gather 'round, with nectar near,
In pollen's jest, we have no fear.
For nature's verse, so light and free,
Brings smiles and giggles, endlessly!

Canvases of the Quiet Grove

In a grove where silence paints,
The trees gossip, playing saints.
They whisper secrets, giggle low,
As leaves rustle, putting on a show.

A rabbit winks, his art's unique,
With doodles made of carrot cheek.
He draws with joy, yet spills some paint,
And suddenly, oh! He's quite the saint!

The badger's brush is slick and bold,
But splatters colors, uncontrolled.
He swears it's art, our guffaws rise,
As everyone laughs at his muddy ties.

Yet in this grove, where joy is sown,
Each canvas tells the stories grown.
For laughter blooms where art is wild,
In every stroke, there's humor filed!

Imagery of Intertwining Vines

In a tangle of green, a snail lost his way,
He pondered his choices, from night until day.
The vines all around, they giggled and swayed,
While he wore a frown, utterly dismayed.

A squirrel in a tie, with acorns to sell,
Said, "Buy one, get none! It's a bargain, oh swell!"
The vines seemed to chuckle, all twisty and taut,
As the squirrel tried haggling, he soon lost the thought.

The daisies all danced, wearing hats made of cheer,
The vines whispered secrets that only they hear.
A rogue bumblebee buzzed in, striking a pose,
But tripped on a petal, and fell on his nose.

So when you're out walking, just lighten your load,
Among tangled vines, there's a whimsical road.
For nature's a jester, with jokes to bestow,
In a world of such laughter, just let your heart glow!

Poems by the Dappled Sunlight.

Under the branches, the sunlight rays play,
A frog in a crown sings a silly ballet.
The daisies all chuckle, as shadows parade,
While the sun beams a grin, in a light-hearted way.

A hedgehog with glasses, reciting a sonnet,
Said, "Insects, dear friends, you won't find a bonnet!"
The sun gave a wink, with a flicker of light,
While the hedgehog spun tales, taking flight with delight.

In patches of gold, the grasshoppers leap,
Practicing their dance, without time for sleep.
The sun giggles softly, teasing things near,
As a rabbit in shorts prances—how silly, oh dear!

So frolic in sunlight, where laughter does bloom,
In the wild of the forest, where absurdity looms.
A gathering of joy, a whimsical spree,
Under dappled rays, it's a dreamy jubilee!

Whispers of the Forest Grove

In the heart of the grove, the trees share a joke,
A wise old oak chuckles, then starts to poke.
With acorns a-falling, they scatter around,
While a rabbit in slippers hops high off the ground.

The ferns do a dance, as the brook sings a song,
While the critters all gather to sing along.
A parakeet squawks, "Is this party for me?"
And the mushrooms all giggle, "Just wait, you will see!"

A fox in a cloak reads a tale quite absurd,
Of a dragon who fancied himself quite a bird.
The trees lean in closer, they whisper and sigh,
As the squirrel chimes in, "He could nearly fly!"

So listen to whispers, in the woods when you roam,
Where laughter and stories create a sweet home.
In a forest of mirth, let your worries disperse,
For the charm of the grove turns life into verse!

Echoes Beneath the Canopy

Beneath leafy arches, a chorus does sing,
A raccoon in pajamas says, "Where's my bling?"
The echoes bounce back, with a giggle and sway,
While the sunlight performs, in its own silly play.

A fox and a mouse team up for a quest,
To find out who's fastest in this feathered fest.
The trees hold their breath, as they peek through the leaves,
While the critters all cheer, "Oh, what a surprise!"

A snail in a shell says, "I'm winning, you see,"
While the others just giggle and shout, "Let's agree!"
The forest is buzzing with laughter and mirth,
As echoes of fun dance throughout the earth.

So join in the laughter, let your spirit roam free,
In the joy of the woods, where there's always a spree.
In echoes of nature, let your heart sing loud,
For beneath the tall trees, you're part of the crowd!

Tales of Twilit Wildflowers

In the meadow where daisies dance,
The bees wear hats, quite by chance.
They buzz a tune, a cheerful song,
While bugs play chess the whole day long.

A butterfly sipping tea, oh my!
It spills on ants, who laugh and cry.
The flowers gossip with a grin,
About the squirrels and their acorn sin.

At dusk the crickets start their play,
They form a band and sway away.
With twinkling lights, fireflies glow,
Inviting all to join their show.

When night descends, a raccoon sings,
Of moonlit games and funny things.
So come and dance, let laughter swell,
In twilit fields where stories dwell.

The Chronicle of Quiet Streams

Down by the brook, the fish tell tales,
Of frogs in hats, and merry snails.
They host a party, water balloons,
With giggles echoing 'neath the moons.

A turtle beats a bongo drum,
While salmon wiggle just for fun.
The splashy jokes make ripples loud,
Inviting even the shyest crowd.

A heron drops his fancy tie,
As he attempts to learn to fly.
With every flop, the others cheer,
The laughter spreads from ear to ear.

At dusk, they toast with cups of dew,
Recalling all their antics, too.
In quiet streams, the fun is clear,
With nature's cheer, we all draw near.

Verses of the Ethereal Grove

In a grove where the shadows play,
The squirrels prance in a cheeky way.
They juggle acorns, up in the trees,
While owls hoot jokes with expert ease.

The wind whispers secrets to the leaves,
As rabbits wear their best, bright weaves.
Mice on skateboards zoom and glide,
While foxes cheer from the grassy side.

Beneath the stars, the fun ignites,
With dancing fireflies, oh what sights!
A badger breaks out in a jig,
While hedgehogs giggle, calling big.

So if you're lost, just take a peek,
In this grove, it's joy we seek.
With laughter echoing through the night,
Every creature joins the delight.

The Heartbeat of Hidden Hollows

In hidden nooks where shadows grow,
The rabbits play tag, oh what a show!
They race through ferns, with cheeks all full,
While chipmunks cheer, in this woodland school.

A wise old owl, with glasses on,
Reads silly tales from dusk 'til dawn.
With every word, the forest laughs,
The grumpy badger shares his gaffs.

The brook babbles jokes, oh what a treat,
As turtles join in with their slow beat.
Frogs throw a dance, in modern style,
And every stomp draws out a smile.

Under the stars, they gather 'round,
With giggles and joy, their hearts unbound.
In hidden hollows, magic thrives,
Where humor lives and laughter thrives.

Chants from the Thicket's Heart

The squirrel has a secret stash,
With acorns piled in quite a mash.
He guards them well, oh what a hoot,
While birds all tease and give a toot.

A chipmunk sings of summer's cheer,
While ants march by, they just can't hear.
The thicket's buzz is full of jest,
Where laughter lives, it's simply best.

In shadows deep, where echoes play,
A fox tells tales of yesterday.
With wagging tails and winking eyes,
They spin tall tales beneath the skies.

The owl throws a party, all in white,
With mice as guests, it's quite a fright.
They dance and prance, oh what a scene,
With moonlight glinting, it's quite the sheen.

Verses of the Twilight Grove

In twilight's glow, the rabbits hop,
They stopped to rhyme, then took a drop.
The fireflies flicker as they play,
While crickets join the fun, hooray!

A badger grins with muddy paws,
And counts the stars without a pause.
"Oh look!" he laughs, "I've found a moon,
But it's just cheese – I'll eat it soon!"

The hedgehog rolls, a prickly ball,
And wobbles round, he'll never fall.
He stumbles near a sleeping doe,
And whispers jokes from long ago.

As night unfolds with shadows long,
The grove bursts forth with silly song.
Each creature shares a hearty laugh,
In twilight's arms, they find their path.

Scribbles in a Sunbeam

A sunbeam shines on paper leaves,
Where ants write tales with tiny sheaves.
They scribble words of jam and pies,
In hopes the world will hear their cries.

A dancing frog jumps to the beat,
And sings of flies to make it sweet.
The lizards cheer with zippy tunes,
While butterflies chase away the moons.

With crayon minds, the bugs all draw,
A picture book that stirs in awe.
The beetle sketches a grand parade,
Where all join in, a grand charade!

Then twilight snaps the sun away,
And all the scribbles start to play.
In dusk's embrace, they find their glee,
With every line, it's pure esprit!

The Rhyme of Rustling Leaves

The leaves whisper secrets in the breeze,
With giggles and chuckles that always tease.
"Oh, watch your head!" cries a grateful crow,
"If you don't duck, you'll never know!"

The raccoon jests with twinkling eyes,
"Let's make a cake, and it'll surprise!"
But as he stirs with paws so small,
The batter spills, and he takes a fall!

Two toads debate near the river's chime,
Who can catch flies in the fastest time?
With flicks and flops, they leap so high,
While ducks quack loud and cannot lie.

As dusk approaches, shadows dance,
Each creature joins in a merry prance.
In rustling leaves, the fun won't cease,
Where nature's laughter finds its peace.

Briars and Ballads

In tangled thorns, a ballad strays,
The rabbits dance in clumsy ways.
A hedgehog hums a silly tune,
While owls glance down, oh what a boon!

A mischievous fox tells jokes at night,
The fireflies play with flickering light.
Snakes slide by to hear the fun,
Charmed by tales that never run!

In this patch where laughter grows,
Even the shyest critter knows,
To join the chorus, loud and bright,
With chirps and squeaks, they own the night!

So grab your friends, it's time to sing,
Celebrate all that nature brings.
With briars twisting, fun won't cease,
In this wild place, we find our peace!

Cadence of the Conifers

The pines sway gently with a beat,
While squirrels spin in ruffled feet.
Laughter echoes through the pine,
As acorns fall, oh what a sign!

Each needle whispers a clever jest,
While chipmunks pause, they never rest.
The melody of rustling leaves,
A concert hall that nature weaves!

Branches tap like a playful band,
As ants march forth, a tiny hand.
In this grove, no time to pout,
With bouncy tunes, there's no doubt!

Join in the dance, let laughter soar,
In the conifers, you'll find much more.
A cadence bright, a quirky flow,
In nature's grip, let giggles grow!

The Poetry of Pinecones

Pinecones gather, a quirky crowd,
Beneath the trees, they're feeling proud.
Each one tells a silly tale,
Of woodland critters brave and pale.

A squirrel recites with flair and grace,
While the wise owl shares a secret place.
With every roll, a giggle unfurls,
Nature's poets, adorned in swirls!

With humor stitched in bark and seed,
The forest thrives on laughter's creed.
Come join the fest, let spirits fly,
As echoes bounce from tree to sky!

Together they weave a playful rhyme,
In every nook, throughout all time.
With pinecones scattered here and there,
We laugh out loud without a care!

Reflections of the Resilient

Amidst the trees, reflections glow,
Of creatures wise with hearts aglow.
A toad croaks out a hearty cheer,
While bees gather, drawing near.

The brook laughs softly, bubbling clear,
Whispering jokes for all to hear.
With stones adorned in mossy gleams,
Nature thrives on silly dreams!

Each twig and leaf partakes in jest,
Finding joy in every quest.
So gather round, take heed, my friend,
In nature's fun, there's no end!

Resilience here is full of spark,
With every joke that lights the dark.
In laughter found from roots to leaves,
Life's quirks abound, and joy retrieves!

The Quiet Quatrain of Quakes

In a forest filled with giggling trees,
A squirrel tripped and landed on his knees.
The mushrooms laughed with their little caps,
While the bushes whispered of all the mishaps.

A deer waltzed in with two left feet,
The owl hooted jokes, oh, so sweet.
Bouncing rabbits joined in the fun,
Chasing shadows until they're done.

An acorn dropped with a thud so bold,
The clever fox joked, 'Look, it's pure gold!'
But the wise old tortoise took his time,
Said laughter's what makes the woods so sublime.

So come gather 'round in this joyful glade,
Where every blunder becomes a parade.
With giggles echoing under the sun,
In this forest, mischief is never done.

Ink-stained Petals

In the garden where the daisies write,
Petals spill ink in the warm sunlight.
A bee buzzes in, looking for a snack,
While roses pester, 'Hey, don't look back!'

The tulips conspire with their colors bright,
'Let's paint the fence, it feels just right!'
With brush and whimsy, they start to play,
As the wind carries their laughter far away.

A daffodil tripped, fell into the ink,
Smeared on its face, gave the whole thing a wink.
The butterflies giggled, oh, what a scene,
While the violets chimed in, all fresh and clean.

So rally the blooms for a fanciful spree,
Shake off the dirt, let the fun be free!
In this garden of giggles, life's just a jest,
With ink-stained petals, we're truly blessed.

Harmonies of the Hidden Hollow

In the hollow where the critters sing,
A raccoon danced, wearing a shiny ring.
The frogs croaked out a comedic tune,
While rabbits boogied beneath the moon.

A fox with flair played the bongo beats,
As chipmunks snapped their tiny little feets.
A shy hedgehog joined with his prickle pride,
Creating a rhythm from side to side.

A turtle lagged behind with a slow groove,
But when he got moving, the whole crowd moved.
Laughter erupted with each little blunder,
In this hidden spot full of joyful wonder.

So spin and twirl, join the creature band,
Let mischief and music go hand in hand.
In the hidden hollow where giggles flow,
Each harmony crafted sets spirits aglow.

Phrasing the Pathless Path

On a path where no one quite knows where to go,
A hedgehog and rabbit put on quite a show.
They twirled and twisted, went round and round,
With every misstep, more giggles they found.

The trees peeked in, enjoying the dance,
Swaying their branches, giving cheers a chance.
The pheasants clucked, craving the glee,
"Let's join the fun, it's wild and free!"

A lost little mouse tried to make it quite clear,
Map in his paws, filled with crumbs and cheer.
But as he got tangled in grass, what a sight!
He laughed and exclaimed, "I'm never alright!"

So wander these woods with a chuckle and grin,
For every wrong turn, a laugh can begin.
In the world of the lost, find joy as your path,
And let every stumble bring forth the best laugh.

The Ballad of the Broken Branch

A branch once dreamed to reach the sky,
But tripped on roots and gave a sigh.
It whispered tales of birds' missed flights,
And giggled with the glowfire lights.

The squirrels laughed, they couldn't wait,
To claim their throne on this fallen fate.
A swing for all, a makeshift ride,
This broken limb, their silly pride.

The flowers danced, the grass would sway,
As laughter echoed, they'd refuse to play.
For nature's whims can break and bend,
And every story brings a friend.

So next you stroll through trees so tall,
Listen closely for the call.
You might just hear the giggles rise,
From a branch beneath the bright blue skies.

Penning Nature's Prose

In bushes green where scribes do hide,
An ink-stained frog hops with delight.
He drafts his tales with lily pens,
And dreams of fish and foam-filled dens.

A cricket chirps, a wise old sage,
Reciting poetry, turning the page.
He frets that squirrels can't hold their prose,
As they forget how rhymes should flow.

The kindly owl, with glasses set,
Watches the scene and starts to fret.
His wisdom hides behind her flaps,
While laughing at the squirrel's mishaps.

So wander in the realms of green,
Where frogs and crickets have their scene.
Embrace the chaos, join the fun,
For nature's tales are never done.

Songs of the Shadowed Thicket

In dim-lit nooks where shadows play,
A raccoon hosts a cabaret.
With acorn hats and berry shoes,
He charms the crowd as night ensues.

The owls hoot in a rhythmic beat,
While fireflies dance and find their seat.
The hedgehogs munch on snappy tunes,
And groove beneath the silver moons.

A fawn joins in, with clumsy grace,
Her prancing dance, a wild chase.
Giggles echo through the thick,
As laughter weaves the woodland's trick.

So come and twirl in leafy nests,
With critters who are simply the best.
Embrace the joy of night's delight,
In thickets dark, where dreams take flight.

Stanzas in the Sunlight

Beneath the sun, a picnic spread,
Where ants and beetles fear to tread.
A rabbit hops, forgetting lunch,
And squirrels giggle, on a munch.

The daisies sway, they know the rhyme,
Tickling bees with nectar trim.
While wise old trees, with bark so bold,
Share secrets of the tales of old.

A frolicsome fox joins this feast,
Stealing snacks like a playful beast.
With every bite, a silly cheer,
As critters come from far and near.

So gather round, let laughter soar,
In sunlight's glow, we'll ask for more.
In grassy fields, let joy be found,
For nature's fun knows no bounds.

Sonnet of the Stream

A fish once tried to wear a hat,
But it slipped into the water flat.
A frog jumped in, said, "What a clown!"
Then danced around, in pure renown.

The otter laughed, began to cheer,
Claimed, "In this stream, we hold a leer!"
The turtles joined, they sang a tune,
And bubbles danced beneath the moon.

A duck quacked loud, with feathers bright,
"This stream is where we take delight!"
While dragonflies buzzed overhead,
They chuckled 'bout the fish instead.

So in this stream, the fun won't cease,
Where critters share their jokes with ease.
And every splash, a laugh does bring,
As nature's court begins to sing.

Metaphors Among the Moss

Among the moss, they sit and think,
With thoughts that rarely make a wink.
A squirrel says, "I'm quite profound!"
While munching nuts upon the ground.

A hedgehog speaks in riddles strange,
His quills all shiny, quite deranged.
The toadstools nod, in silent glee,
As nature's jesters roam so free.

Each metaphor, a silly sight,
A worm once dreamed of taking flight!
But found too late, his charm was lost,
As friends just laughed, "You paid the cost!"

Beneath the trees, they love to jest,
No woodland party could be less blessed.
In mossy nooks, they share their lore,
Where echoes of laughter live and soar.

Reflections in the Riverrun

In the riverrun, a beaver brags,
While wearing tiny, fashionable tags.
He builds a dam with style and flair,
And all the fish just stop and stare.

A turtle grins, with a wink and nod,
Claimed he's a marathon champ, by God!
But all he does is plod along,
With mossy ears that can't hear wrong.

A heron struts, like he's the queen,
While ripples ripple, and fish convene.
"Catch me if you can!" they shout with glee,
But they just tease, under the leafy spree.

Thus, in the riverrun, laughter flows,
Where every critter fully knows,
That fun is found in silly deeds,
To swim and splash—fulfilling needs!

Fables from the Forest Floor

Beneath the leaves, a tale unfolds,
Of creatures brave and stories bold.
A wise old owl, with spectacles keen,
Gathers young ones for sights unseen.

A raccoon, dressed with flair so fine,
Claims he can dance, but it's more like a line.
The others laugh, without a care,
As he twirls around, flipping his hair.

A badger brings a pie made of mud,
Insisting it's sweet, while calling it "Stud!"
The critters scrunch their noses tight,
"Oh dear, that's quite a terrible sight!"

So from the forest floor they share,
The fables spun with laughter in air.
Where each tall tale brings a smile to the face,
In this magical, silly place.

Sagas of the Swamp

In the murky depths where frogs convene,
With tales of jest and antics unseen.
The gators gossip, the turtles snicker,
In this soggy land, where life is quicker.

A raccoon stole a shiny old shoe,
He wore it proudly, a sight quite askew.
The herons flutter, with feathers in fluff,
As laughter erupts, oh this swamp's got the stuff!

The fireflies blink in a dance that's absurd,
As a beaver croons, oh haven't you heard?
An otter recounts his great fight with a stick,
While the cattails chuckle, "What's up with that trick?"

So gather, dear friends, in the marshy delight,
With pranks and with puns, it's a comedic night.
In the sagas we share, the joy won't be stifled,
For laughter's our treasure, our swamp-like delight!

Eulogies of the Evergreens

Amidst the pines where the squirrels conspire,
A gathering blooms, with jokes to inspire.
The wind whispers secrets, a giggling breeze,
As needles drop down, just like stories from trees.

"Remember that time," a fir echoes with glee,
"When I wore a scarf made of spaghetti!"
The spruces all chuckle, with laughter they sway,
In this forest of fun, where spirits play.

One cedar once claimed he could dance like a fox,
But tripped on a root, fell right in a box!
With giggles and snorts, they regale all the lore,
Of timber and tussles, and much more in store.

The eulogies shared bring a smile to the bark,
For life in the trees has a whimsical spark.
So raise up a glass—of the sap, don't you dare!
For the evergreens' humor is a treasure we share!

The Epistle of the Evening

As dusk draws near, and the critters align,
An owl pens a letter, a tale so divine.
"Dear Moon, you shine, like a lantern in flight,
While bats practice flip-flops, oh what a sight!"

The badger adds notes, with whiskers all twitchy,
"Don't forget about dinner, we feast rather kitschy!
With berry-filled pies and a splash of sweet tea,
Let's celebrate quirks, wild and free as can be!"

Fireflies flicker, like stars on the ground,
While bunnies hop in, with thumps all around.
"Dear friends, let's toast to our merry old crew,
With zany adventures, oh what will we do?"

In this evening epistle, camaraderie glows,
With laughter and joy that every heart knows.
So gather, dear friends, as the night drifts away,
For the tales we create will forever play!

Whimsy Among the Willows

By the river's edge where the willows sway,
There's mischief afoot in the light of the day.
A duck in a tux, quacking tunes like a star,
While the fish in the pond applaud from afar.

A rabbit with glasses is reading a book,
Tucked under a tree with a nonsensical hook.
The frogs hop along, in a dance oh so bright,
While squirrels throw acorns in playful delight.

"Oh dear willow," hums one with a grin,
"Share me your shadow, I'm losing, I win!"
The grasses all giggle, the breeze plays a part,
In this jolly jest, they all win at the art!

So come join the frolic, let worries take flight,
In the whimsy of willows, where laughter feels right.
With friends all around, there's nothing to rue,
For the joy in these antics is a treasure so true!

The Scribe of the Silent Woods

In the forest, where branches sway,
A squirrel types on a gleaming tray.
He giggles at tales of the fawns,
Drafting tales of magical lawns.

The owls hoot at his playful prose,
While rabbits dance on their tiny toes.
A porcupine writes with a quill,
His poetry gives all a thrill.

His ink is made from berries bright,
He scribbles stories late at night.
With each word, the woods come alive,
In laughter, all creatures thrive.

Next, he pens a tale for the bees,
About honey and flowers that tease.
So gather 'round, join in the fun,
For the scribe's work is never done!

Odes to the Oak

Oh mighty oak, with branches wide,
You boast of acorns, what a pride!
Squirrels hoard them for winter's bite,
While chipmunks giggle, oh, what a sight!

Your bark's a canvas—what a mess,
With carvings of love, none the less.
You sway and creak in the breeze,
Making the forest laugh with ease.

The birds compose tunes on your limbs,
While beneath, the moles hum sweet hymns.
Even the bugs join in the fun,
Dancing around till day is done.

So here's to the oak, grand and stout,
With stories whispered all about.
May your shade bring joy, laughter, and cheer,
As you stand tall through every year!

Verses at Dusk

As twilight descends, critters unite,
Telling tall tales in fading light.
A fox regales with tales of the hunt,
While badgers clap, shouting, "Aunt! Aunt!"

The fireflies twinkle, adding some flair,
Their glow a spotlight on woodland air.
A raccoon struts, telling jokes quite absurd,
The trees seem to chuckle at every word.

With leaves as their stage, and stars overhead,
They laugh till they stumble, then head off to bed.
Each night a new chapter, what could be more?
'Round the campfire, the stories will soar.

So gather your friends, come join this delight,
With verses at dusk, everything feels right.
The woods are alive, with laughter and cheer,
Making each night bright as dawn draws near.

The Bark Beneath My Words

On tree trunks, I carve my little verse,
Where squirrels giggle, and it's quite diverse.
"Why did the pine tree sit in a chair?"
"Because it wanted to get some fresh air!"

My words echo through roots and leaves,
As the forest chuckles and heartily heaves.
A hedgehog snickers, rolling in glee,
"Can trees talk? Well, let's wait and see!"

With every chisel, a new laugh is born,
As chipmunks laugh till the break of dawn.
The bark's my canvas, my truth to share,
In this cheerful realm, without a care.

So come hear the whispers of laughter and joy,
From each creature, gal, and every boy.
For under the stars, my stories unfold,
Just like the treasures from the forest of old!

Ballads of the Swaying Canopy

Leaves gossip above, what a tale to tell,
A squirrel in tights, dancing quite well.
Branches twist and bend, like a contorted jam,
A symphony of branches, oh what a scheme, wham!

The wind sings along, a playful breeze's tune,
While owls hoot in laughter, beneath the bright moon.
A pogo stick fern, jumps with both glee,
As laughter spills forth, from each singing tree.

The acorns roll over, in jolly parade,
A nutty anthem played, never to fade.
Dancing through shadows, in joyous delight,
A woodland ballet, from morning to night.

So come hear the giggles, where the tall trees squawk,
With whispers of fun, as the branches rock.
Nature's odd parties, where all are invited,
In ballads of joy, forever ignited.

Secrets in the Sapling's Sigh

Saplings chuckle low, secrets they keep,
Whispering sweet nothings, before they sleep.
A beetle with glasses reads poetry slow,
While the ferns roll their eyes, with a silent 'whoa!'

Oh the tales they weave, of frog princes lost,
A trio of fungi, who win at all cost.
Mossy memoirs sprout, in shades of green glow,
As they laugh at the sky, not a care in tow.

A twig with a wig claims royal decree,
Perhaps it's a branch with an identity spree.
Giggling to blossoms, they throw a grand ball,
Dancing in circles, they're having a ball!

Secrets exchanged, in a rustling tune,
Who knew that young saplings could be such a boon?
With laughter and whimsy, they whisper their style,
In saplings' soft breezes, let's stay for a while.

Phrases from the Forest Floor

Beneath the tall trunks, where shadows sneak,
The floor fills with giggles, the trees all speak.
Mushrooms gather round for a very loud chat,
While critters in coats exchange silly hats.

The underbrush chuckles, a humorous sight,
With crickets composing a song every night.
A hedgehog recites lines from the old, dusty lore,
As the daisies burst forth in a riotous roar.

The grumpy old roots grumble beneath,
Telling tall tales of wonderful heath.
Rogue dandelions shoot off in glee,
Spinning wild stories for all who can see.

In whispers they share, in the quiet below,
With riddles and rhymes, to and fro they go.
A treasure of phrases, from the forest floor,
Where laughter is endless, forever once more!

Rhythms of the Nightingale's Nest

Nightingales giggle, with wings wide apart,
Creating sweet rhythms, a laugh from the heart.
Sticks in a bundle, building quite high,
With a frog as their DJ, oh my, oh my!

"Tweet-tweet!" goes the chorus, in playful refrain,
As fireflies twinkle, like the stars in the rain.
An owl in confusion wears spectacles tight,
While the night ditty dances, a marvelous sight.

Swinging from branches, in laughter's embrace,
A nightingale's jig becomes quite the chase.
With shadows that sway, and costumes of light,
Jamming in harmony until morning is bright.

So join in the fun, let the music compel,
Under stars that shine bright, oh can you tell?
The rhythms of laughter, in every soft nest,
With nightingales singing, we all feel so blessed.

www.ingramcontent.com/pod-product-compliance
Lightning Source LLC
Chambersburg PA
CBHW071822160426
43209CB00003B/177